A MACDONALD BOOK
Copyright © 1985 Arnoldo Mondadori Editore S.p.A.,
Milan
Translated from the Italian by Penny Mishcon
Editor: Philip Steele
Design: Sally Boothroyd

First published in Great Britain in 1985 by
Macdonald & Co. (Publishers) Ltd.
London & Sydney

A member of BPCC plc

ISBN 0 356 11233 0

Macdonald & Co. (Publishers) Ltd.,
Maxwell House,
74, Worship Street,
London EC2A 2EN

Printed and bound in Spain by Artes Graficas Toledo S.A.
D. L. TO: 1561 -1984

Ceserani, Paolo
    In search of Pompeii.
    1. Pompeii (Ancient city)—Antiquities—
    Juvenile literature   2. Italy—Antiquities
    —Juvenile literature
    I. Title   II. Ventura, Piero
    937′.7   DG70.P7

    ISBN 0-356-11233-0

IN SEARCH OF
POMPEII

Piero Ventura and Gian Paolo Ceserani

Macdonald

Contents

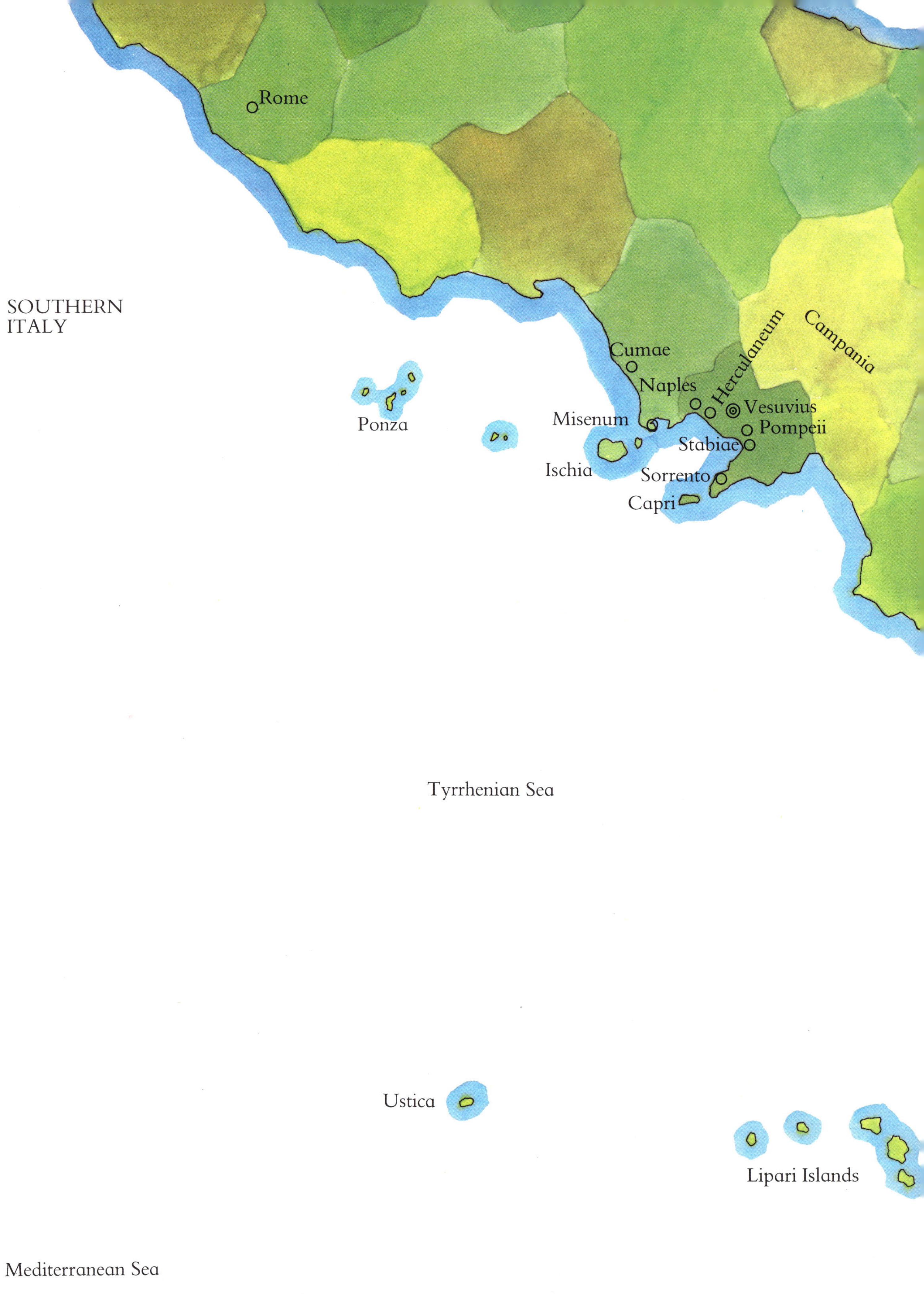

SOUTHERN
ITALY

○Rome

Cumae ○
Naples ○
Herculaneum
Campania
◎ Vesuvius
Misenum ○
Pompeii ○
Ponza
Stabiae ○
Sorrento ○
Ischia
Capri

Tyrrhenian Sea

Ustica

Lipari Islands

Mediterranean Sea

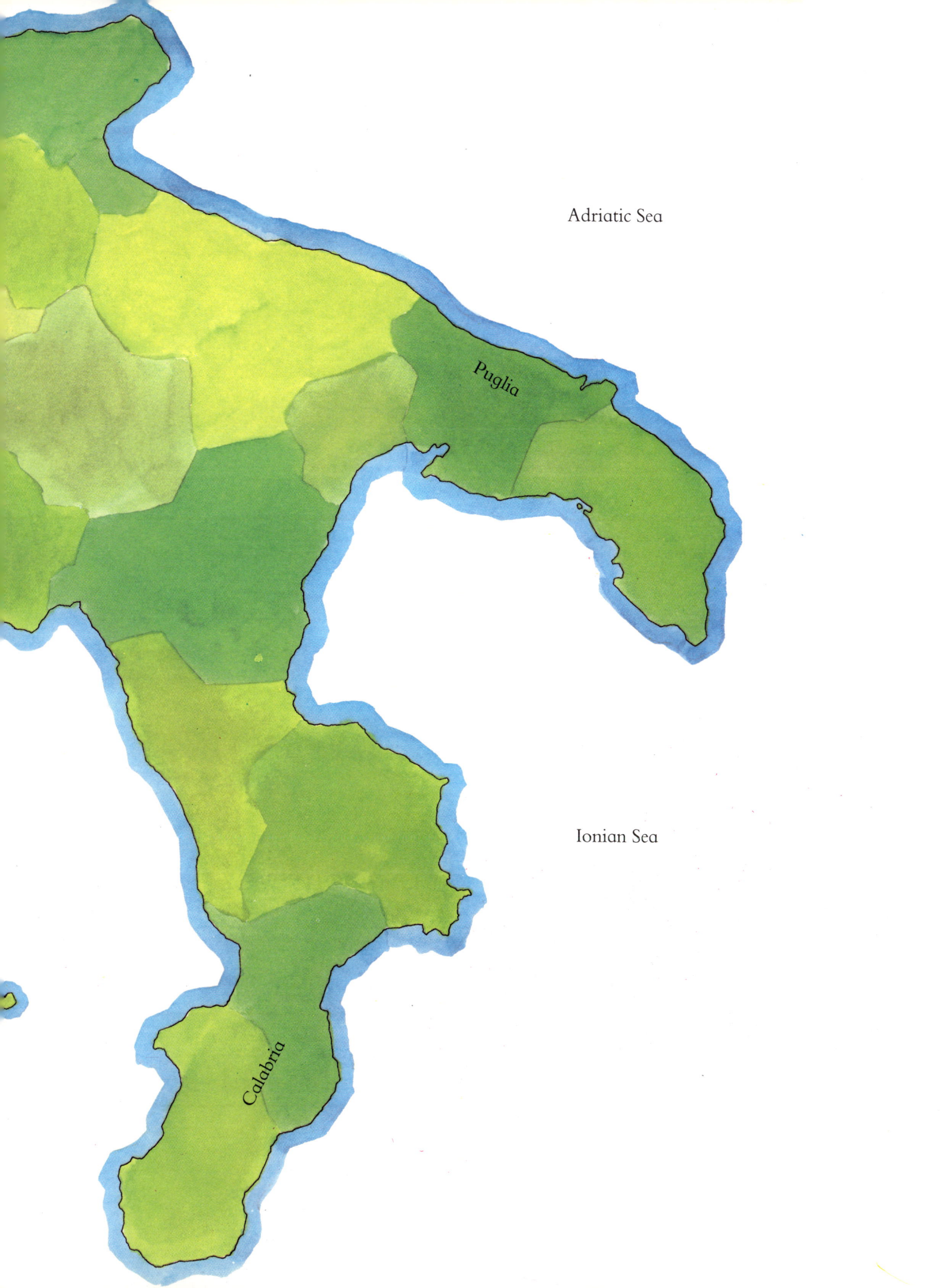

Adriatic Sea

Puglia

Ionian Sea

Calabria

Treasure trove

One day in February 1748 a poor farmer was ploughing a field. He lived in the countryside near Naples, in southern Italy. It was a hilly region. Only a short distance away were the steep slopes of the volcano, Vesuvius.

Like many local people, the farmer lived in fear of Vesuvius. Every so often the volcano would rumble and smoke. If it erupted it might destroy the farmland around about. As the farmer watched the ploughshare turn the soil, he suddenly saw the glint of bronze. He had struck buried treasure: the bronze was from the age of ancient Rome, from the city of Pompeii.

Little did the farmer know that over 1500 years earlier, in AD 79, Vesuvius had erupted. The sides of the volcano had fallen in. A great blast had showered the surrounding countryside with ash and pumice (the stone formed in a volcanic eruption). Streams of hot lava had poured from the mountain, destroying everything in their path.

Two cities had been destroyed in the eruption. One was Herculaneum,

engulfed by a layer of mud 30 metres deep. The other was Pompeii, which was buried by the ash and pumice which rained down from the sky. It formed a layer 5 metres deep in many places. Within a few hours some 2,000 people had been killed.

The cities were never rebuilt. Soon everyone had forgotten that they had ever existed. The centuries passed, and the Roman empire disappeared. New people came to live in Italy, and even families who had lived for centuries in the region around Vesuvius knew nothing of the buried cities.

Then in 1710 a villager digging a well uncovered some large marble slabs: he had unearthed the ancient town of Herculaneum. But until 1748 Pompeii remained undiscovered. Today Naples is part of the republic of Italy. In the middle of the 18th century it was a separate kingdom ruled by Charles III. When word of the farmer's discovery reached the king, he was most excited. Excavation of Pompeii began on 25 March 1748, with the king himself looking on.

Almost at once a beautiful wall painting was found, and various metal objects, and human skeletons with gold coins beside them. This was the start of a treasure hunt that was to last for many years. Sadly there was little method in the excavation. There were no scientists involved. There was no system of planning, or careful recording of the objects found.

In 1758 the great German archaeologist Johann Hoachim Winckelmann arrived. The King of Naples made things difficult for Winckelmann. He was jealous and suspicious. When the archaeologist found out the way in which the excavations were being carried out, he was horrified.

Winckelmann's writings on Pompeii were read all over Europe, and the extraordinary story of the buried city became well known. But then tragedy struck. Winckelmann was visiting the city of Trieste, on the Adriatic coast. In the hotel where he was staying he met a man who offered to show him around the town. The man was really a thief, and the next day he attacked and killed Winckelmann.

Kings and queens

Winckelmann was dead, and the excavation of Pompeii was still being organised by greedy and stupid men.

Ferdinand, the young son of Charles III, had become King of Naples. In 1768 Ferdinand IV married Princess Caroline of Austria. He was 17, but he still behaved as if he were a little boy – and a spoilt one at that. He liked to play practical jokes on his courtiers. He would slip pieces of ice into their pockets, and fill their hats with jam.

Ferdinand's only interest was hunting. To keep him happy, deer and boar were kept in enclosures so that he could shoot them at point blank range. Poor Caroline, who was only 15, was desperate at finding herself with such a husband. Her brother, the Emperor Joseph II, visited the court of Naples in an attempt to cheer her up.

Joseph went off on a tour of the kingdom together with his half-witted brother-in-law. When they reached Pompeii Joseph immediately saw the importance of the discovery. He persuaded Ferdinand to have more effort put into the excavation of the site.

Houses, villas and monuments came to light as the soil was cleared. Many skeletons were found. From their positions it was clear that they had died whilst trying to flee from the terrible shower of ashes. The pathetic figures were clutching their most valuable possessions.

The fame of Pompeii spread throughout Europe. Many travellers came to see the site, including kings and princes. A great German poet, Goethe, visited Pompeii and described its streets and houses.

Work on the site was held up for a time by political troubles. By 1808 Naples had another queen called Caroline, sister of the great Napoleon Bonaparte. She became fascinated by Pompeii, and asked for a progress report to be sent to her every day. Scarcely a week went by without her paying a visit to the site.

Eager to please the royal visitor, the workers would cover up objects they had already discovered, only to dig them up again when the queen was there. No serious work could be carried out like this. It was time for a proper excavation.

A city takes shape

The first king to make a united Italy was Victor Emanuel II. He understood the importance of Pompeii, and appointed a man named Giuseppe Fiorelli as director of excavations. Fiorelli, who came from Naples, was a good archaeologist. He put an end to thieving on the site, and in 1861 started a methodical and careful excavation.

Instead of tackling individual houses at random and piling up the rubble carelessly, Fiorelli drew up a plan of the whole town. He opened up buildings from above, to stop them collapsing. Soon it was possible to gain a picture of the different districts of Pompeii, and of the blocks of houses.

Giuseppe Fiorelli worked out a clever way of recording his discoveries. He made plaster casts. Ash and pumice had covered fallen bodies and objects during the eruption. Over the years the bodies became skeletons, but their original shape left behind a hollow in the rock. By filling these hollows with plaster of Paris, Fiorelli brought back to life whole scenes of life in ancient Pompeii.

plaster casts made by Fiorelli

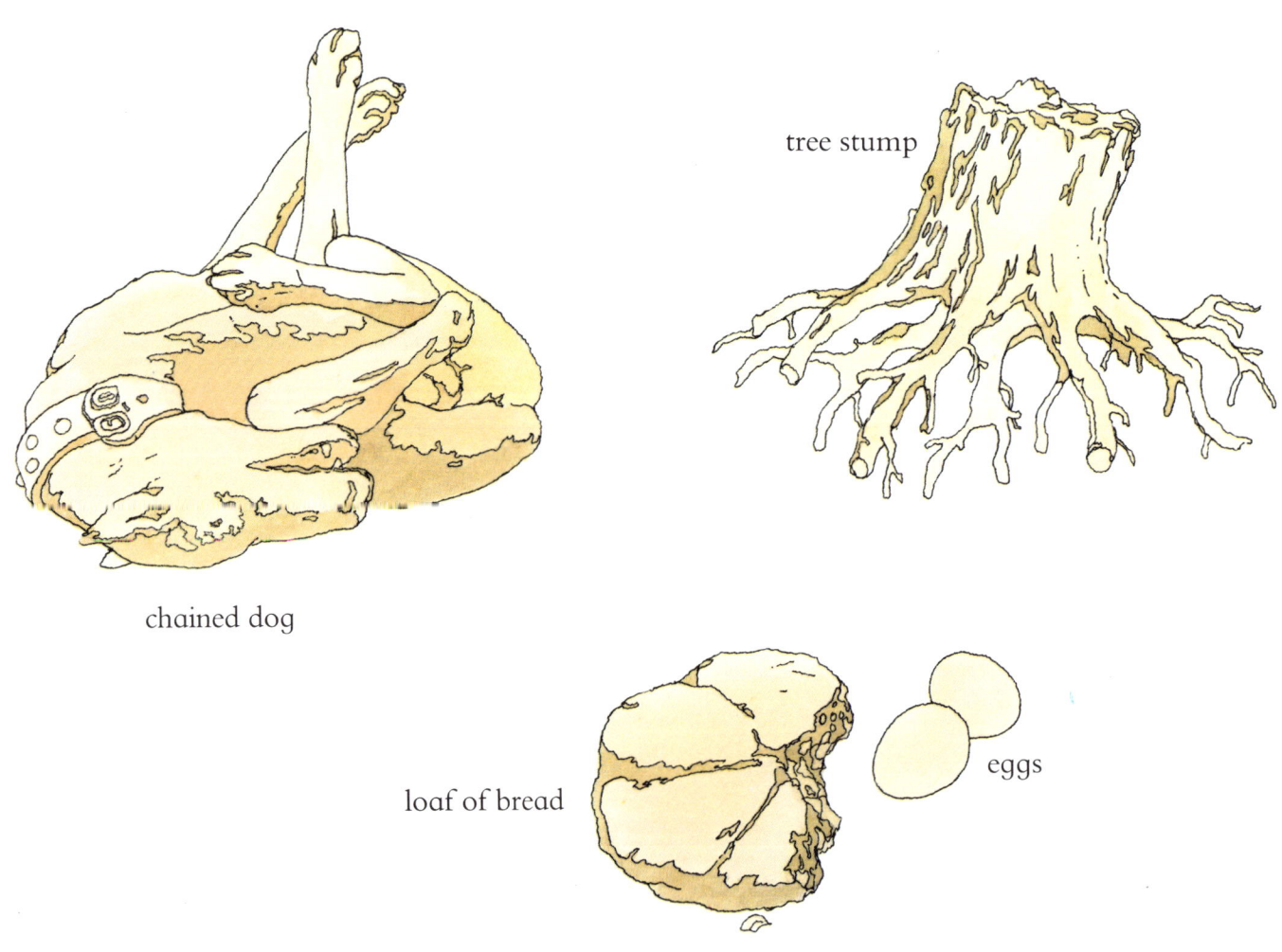

chained dog

tree stump

loaf of bread

eggs

12

1 Pumice and ash rain down on the body of a fleeing Pompeian.

2 Soon the body is completely covered by stones and ash.

3 Long after the body has become a skeleton, its shape remains in the rock.

4 The archaeologist notices the shape and pierces the hollow.

5 Plaster of Paris is carefully poured into the hollow.

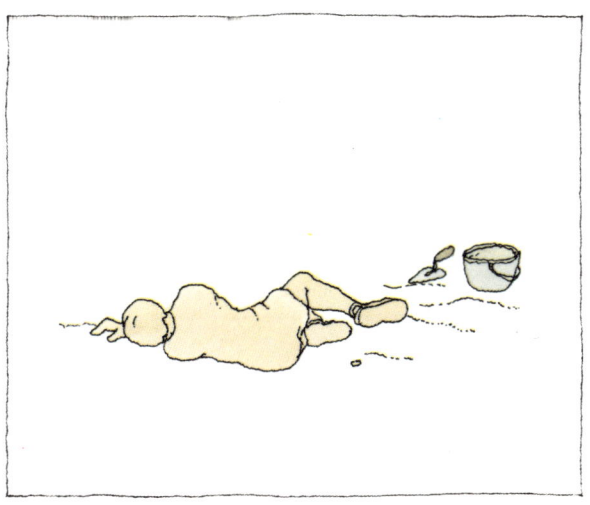

6 When the plaster has hardened it may be dug out of the rock.

Visiting the past

Things have changed since Fiorelli's time. Modern archaeologists can use powerful drills to bore through the hardest layers of lava. Dumper trucks can shift large loads of soil. Aerial photographs can be used to find buried buildings.

Today the excavation of Pompeii is more or less complete. People of the 20th century can stroll through the streets of a town of the first century AD. It is a fascinating experience.

Over the years Pompeii has yielded up a wealth of treasure. In 1831 workers unearthed a beautiful mosaic – a picture made up of tiny coloured fragments. The picture showed one of the heroes of the ancient world, Alexander the Great, at the Battle of Issus in 333 BC.

When the house of the Vettii was excavated in 1894, they even found the bones of meat that was being cooked in the kitchen eighteen centuries earlier! Vases and statues and coins were found, and wall paintings in the Villa of the Mysteries.

Progress on the site has not always been easy. In 1913 a workman discovered a hoard of gold coins and silver vases. He hid the booty and smuggled it abroad, hoping to make a large amount of money for himself. In 1943, during the Second World War, a bomb exploded in the forum, and another one hit the museum. More recently, the city was rocked by an earthquake. But Pompeii has survived – in spite of everything.

15

Ancient Pompeii

Why did people ever decide to build a town on the edge of a volcano? Surely they must have realised how dangerous it was?

The fact was that the soil in the region was very fertile. The lava from past eruptions of Vesuvius had become covered with fine, rich earth in which anything would grow – apples, pears, figs, melons, almonds. The climate was perfect. If you sowed wheat, barley or vegetables you would get two or three crops in a year.

It is hardly surprising that people ignored the dangers of Vesuvius and settled there. The region was first occupied by the people known as

Oscans. They were followed by the Etruscans, the Greeks and the Samnites. By the year 400 BC Pompeii had a population of 3,000. Two centuries later its theatre alone could hold 5,000 spectators.

In 89 BC the city surrendered to Rome after a siege which had lasted a year. It soon became very much a Roman town, and it prospered. However in AD 62 Vesuvius became active, and in a series of earth tremors the buildings of Pompeii were destroyed. This time there was no lava or ash. The city was soon re-built, with splendid villas and monuments. They were to survive for only 17 years.

The city plan

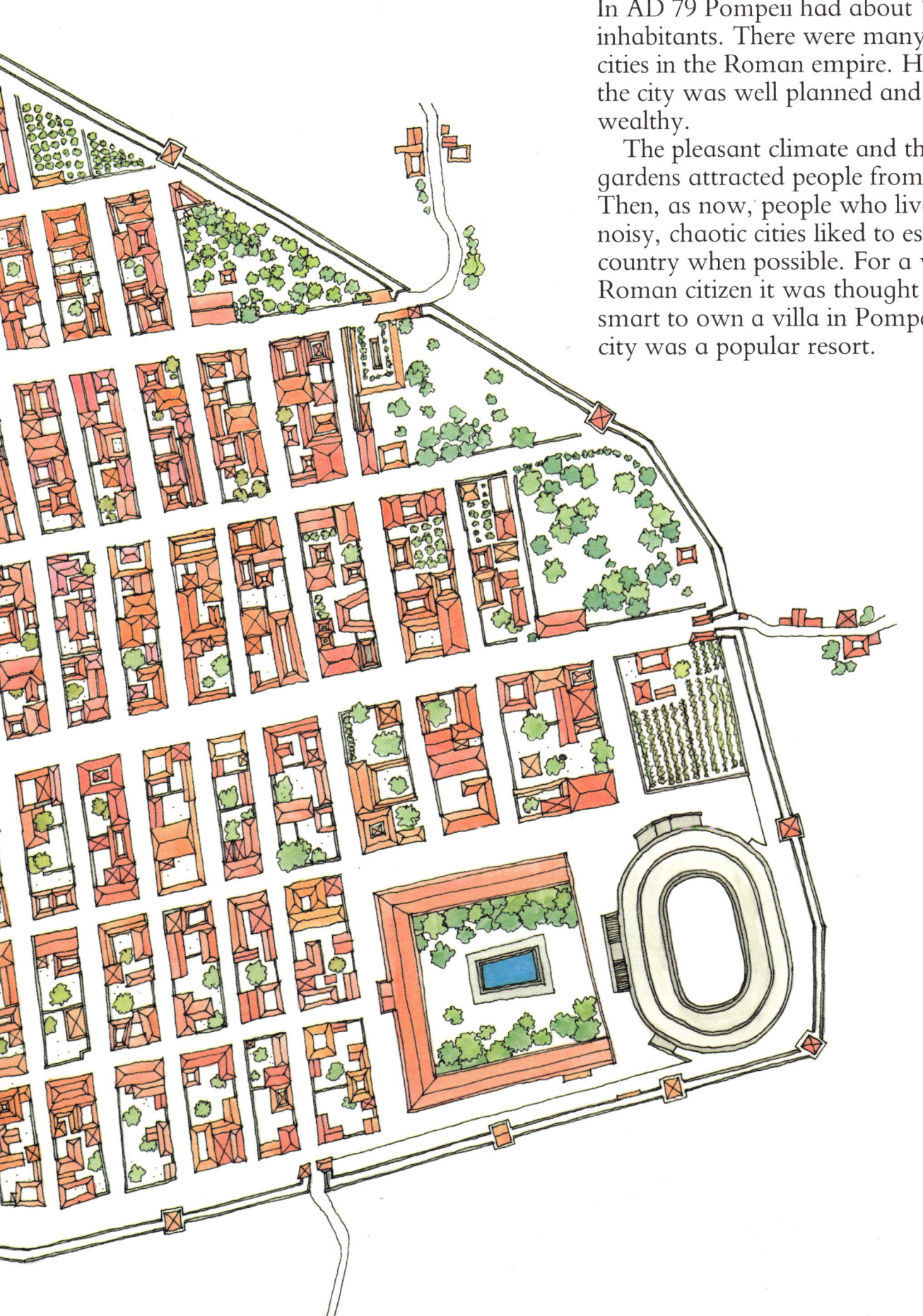

In AD 79 Pompeii had about 15,000 inhabitants. There were many larger cities in the Roman empire. However, the city was well planned and very wealthy.

The pleasant climate and the green gardens attracted people from Rome. Then, as now, people who lived in noisy, chaotic cities liked to escape to the country when possible. For a wealthy Roman citizen it was thought to be very smart to own a villa in Pompeii. The city was a popular resort.

The Forum

Pompeii was a splendid city. In the background were the green slopes of Vesuvius. Beyond the city walls – before the earthquake of AD 62 – there was a view to the blue waters of the sea, sparkling in the sunshine.

As in every Roman city, the forum was at the centre of things. Around a central square were temples, markets, public buildings and law courts. The square was thronged with people, hustling and bustling. Some came to do business, meet lawyers and pay taxes. Others came to meet friends, exchange gossip, or watch the world go by.

The markets were to be found in a covered building paved with marble. Here there were butchers, bakers, fishmongers and greengrocers. You could buy cloth, baskets, lamps, pots, sweets and all kinds of delicacies. The local speciality was a sort of fish sauce. The mild climate meant that Pompeii's markets were often the first with fresh vegetables.

Here too, slaves from all over the empire would be brought and sold. Pompeii was an important centre of trade. Its merchants grew prosperous supplying its citizens with the very latest luxurious goods.

20

Public baths

The Romans were a people who loved to keep themselves clean and trim. Even a small city such as Pompeii had three large public baths, which would suggest that most people bathed once a day.

The baths were rather like a modern sports centre. They included a gymnasium for exercise and an area for games such as bowls. There were massage rooms and a large swimming pool.

The baths themselves included a changing room, a warm room and a hot room, so that one could get used to the temperature gradually. The central heating was a masterpiece of engineering. There were three large tanks – one for the cold water, one for the warm water, and one for the hot. Furnaces were used to heat the water until it turned to steam. The steam was passed under the floors to keep them warm, and passed through vents in the walls and ceilings.

Men and women each had their own sections in the baths. Here they would enjoy a good soak, chatting with friends, discussing business, politics, or the latest scandals in Rome.

The amphitheatre

When it was first built, the amphitheatre at Pompeii was one of the finest in the Roman world. It could hold 20,000 – more than the number of people actually living in the town. People would flock to the amphitheatre from near and far.

The buildings were cleverly designed. The huge crowds were able to leave the stands within a few minutes. An awning could be put up to shade the arena and stands from the sun.

What kinds of games did the ancient Romans enjoy watching? Nothing as gentle as football. The games were cruel and vicious. Slaves and condemned criminals would be forced to fight with lions or to kill each other. The more torture and death, the happier the crowds.

The unfortunate people who fought in the arena were called gladiators. They were trained to fight in a barracks next to the amphitheatre. It was a hard and wretched life, and more often than not a short one.

If at the end of a contest a gladiator was still alive, he would ask for mercy by raising a finger. The crowd would cheer or boo, but it was up to the director of the games to decide. If the gladiator was to be spared, he gave the thumbs-up signal. If the gladiator was to be killed, he gave the thumbs-down.

The men often fought with swords and shields, or with tridents (three-pointed spears) and nets. A good fighter would become a public hero. He might even gain his freedom and become rich. Dreams of such success rarely came true, however. Most gladiators, sooner or later, left the arena dead or maimed.

1 shops
2 kitchen
3 atrium (hall)
4 bedroom
5 study
6 sitting room
7 triclinium (dining room)
8 pantry and store
9 servants' quarters
10 garden

The home

Life in Pompeii was very comfortable if you were wealthy. The plan on the left shows the house of a rich family.

The first thing you will notice is that the rooms are arranged around a large central hall, known in Latin as an *atrium*. This was a covered area, except in the centre where a cistern collected rainwater. A door led into the *atrium* from the street.

Why did all the rooms open inwards rather than on to the street? The answer was noise. We tend to think that only modern cities are noisy, but Pompeii must have been just as bad. Carts would clatter over the cobbles, people would shout, and dogs bark.

At the front of the house, this owner rented out two rooms to be used as shops. At the back of the house a sunny garden offered peace and quiet. Statues and columns surrounded the garden, and indoors the walls would be covered with plaster decorations (stucco) or paintings (frescoes).

Not all Pompeians could afford houses like this. People who were less well off lived in more modest rooms. Only the richest Romans used glass in windows. Most houses had open windows. As a protection against summer heat and winter cold, these were kept very small. Rooms were often very stuffy.

Houses in Pompeii were built from local materials, such as limestone and tuff – the rock made from solidified volcanic ash. The roofs were covered with ridged tiles of clay.

The garden

Bad weather was rare in Pompeii. As one sunny day followed another, it was possible to spend most of the time outdoors. The garden was the coolest place to be.

Pompeian gardens were beautifully laid out. There were fountains and streams, basins of flowers and shady walks. Excavations at Pompeii have shown us which trees were grown: they include fig, pine, cypress, vines and fruit trees.

The gardens were filled with statues and columns. Some had glittering marble discs on them which moved with the wind. In the evening the garden would be lit up with lamps. During the summer meals were usually served out of doors. Since Romans ate lying stretched out on low beds, couches of stone were built in the gardens.

The garden was really part of the house, and its walls were covered with beautiful paintings. Landscapes and pictures of the sea were popular outdoor subjects for artists. Indoors there were often painted patterns, pictures of gods and goddesses, and pictures of flowers and fruit.

oak   cypress   olive   laurel   fig

box   pine   vines   acacia

Pompeian paintings are realistic and use bright colours which are still fresh today. From these paintings we can guess what kind of people lived in the more wealthy homes. They were practical, down to earth people, proud of the riches they had made and eager to display it for all to see.

If you pay a visit to Pompeii today you can still see the colourful wall paintings and the trees and flowers. In the house of the Vettii the garden has been laid out just as it would have been in the first century AD. The sun shines down from the blue sky, and shrubs and bushes cast shadows across the paths. You can almost imagine yourself as an ancient Roman, strolling around the garden with your friends.

A dinner party

The Romans were fond of good food. Some of them were a little too fond of it! Greediness often resulted in them having to send for the doctor. Some wealthy Romans even went bankrupt in their attempts to hold sumptuous banquets for their friends.

A famous Roman writer called Petronius wrote a book called the *Satyricon*. In it he describes a feast at the home of Trimalchio, a rich freedman who wants to show off his new found wealth. The meal seems to go on forever, as one fancy dish follows another.

There is a sow, with a litter of piglets made from marzipan. Two baskets of dates dangle from her tusks. There are thrushes stuffed with raisins, and quinces decorated to look like sea urchins. One dish served up at first looks like a goose surrounded by birds and fishes. In fact it turns out to be made from pieces of stewed meats.

In the *Satyricon* Petronius makes fun of the people at the feast. However, it is easy to see from his book that food was very important to the Romans. The excavations at Pompeii have told us a great deal about their eating habits.

The dining room was normally fairly small. The walls were often covered in paintings or decorations showing

30

different foods. The room was known as the *triclinium*, a word which meant that there were three couches arranged around the table with the food.

The Romans ate lying down. They rested on one elbow and took the food with their right hand. Three people lay on each couch: there were strict rules about this. No meal was held with less than three diners, or with more than nine.

The head of the house lay on the left hand couch, together with his wife and their eldest son. The most important guest lay on the couch nearest to the host. When children were allowed to join in, they were given a small couch at their parents' feet.

The Romans used their hands to eat. They did use spoons, but no forks. Knives were used only in the kitchen, to cut up food. In the kitchen, pots and pans were not so different from the ones we use today.

All kinds of food were eaten by those who could afford it: olives, apples, figs, nuts, mushrooms, cheese, cold or hot meats, fish, game. There was even a kind of stew which you could buy ready-made from certain shops – a sort of Roman take-away! The Romans drank a lot of sweet wine.

Roman food

tableware found at Pompeii

bed

brazier

small table

stool

Everyday objects

Thanks to the archaeologists people now knew how the city was laid out, and how the houses themselves were planned. But what of the furniture and the comforts of everyday life? How much had survived?

Wood had mostly rotted away over the ages. Even so, by using plaster casts archaeologists were able to find out exactly how a Roman bed was made, with a wooden or rope frame. The frescoes on the wall showed what the mattresses looked like, and the covers with their striped patterns.

Many bronze, silver, stone and marble objects had survived at Pompeii.

Gradually the archaeologists were able to piece together the details of everyday life: tables, chairs, couches, cupboards, stools, mirrors, lamps, braziers, combs, needles, jewels.

Many of these objects were like the ones we use today, although sometimes they were used differently. Beds were used for sleeping, of course, in the stuffy, windowless bedrooms. But they were also used for lounging on during the day, or for reading in the study.

Roman houses had little furniture: a few small tables, cupboards, and a few stools and chests. It was not that the Romans led a simple life. The furniture they did have was beautifully made and decorated with gold and silver. The legs of beds and tables were sometimes carved to look like lions' claws.

The small amount of furniture was due to the fact that life in ancient times was never very settled or safe. Wars and plagues were common. You always had to be prepared to gather your possessions together in a hurry and flee. Precious objects were as a rule small. They were kept in strongboxes like the one in the picture.

We can often learn more about the way people used to live by looking at a simple everyday object rather than a piece of precious jewellery. Let us look, by way of example, at the Pompeians' lamps.

Thousands of tiny oil lamps have been found. They are made of bronze or terracotta, and cannot have given out much light on their own. Candles were used too, and candelabras and lampstands to make things brighter.

One lamp was found which could be lowered for reading. This tells us that the Romans were keen readers. This was unusual in ancient times. Not until the 20th century were so many people able to read as in ancient Rome.

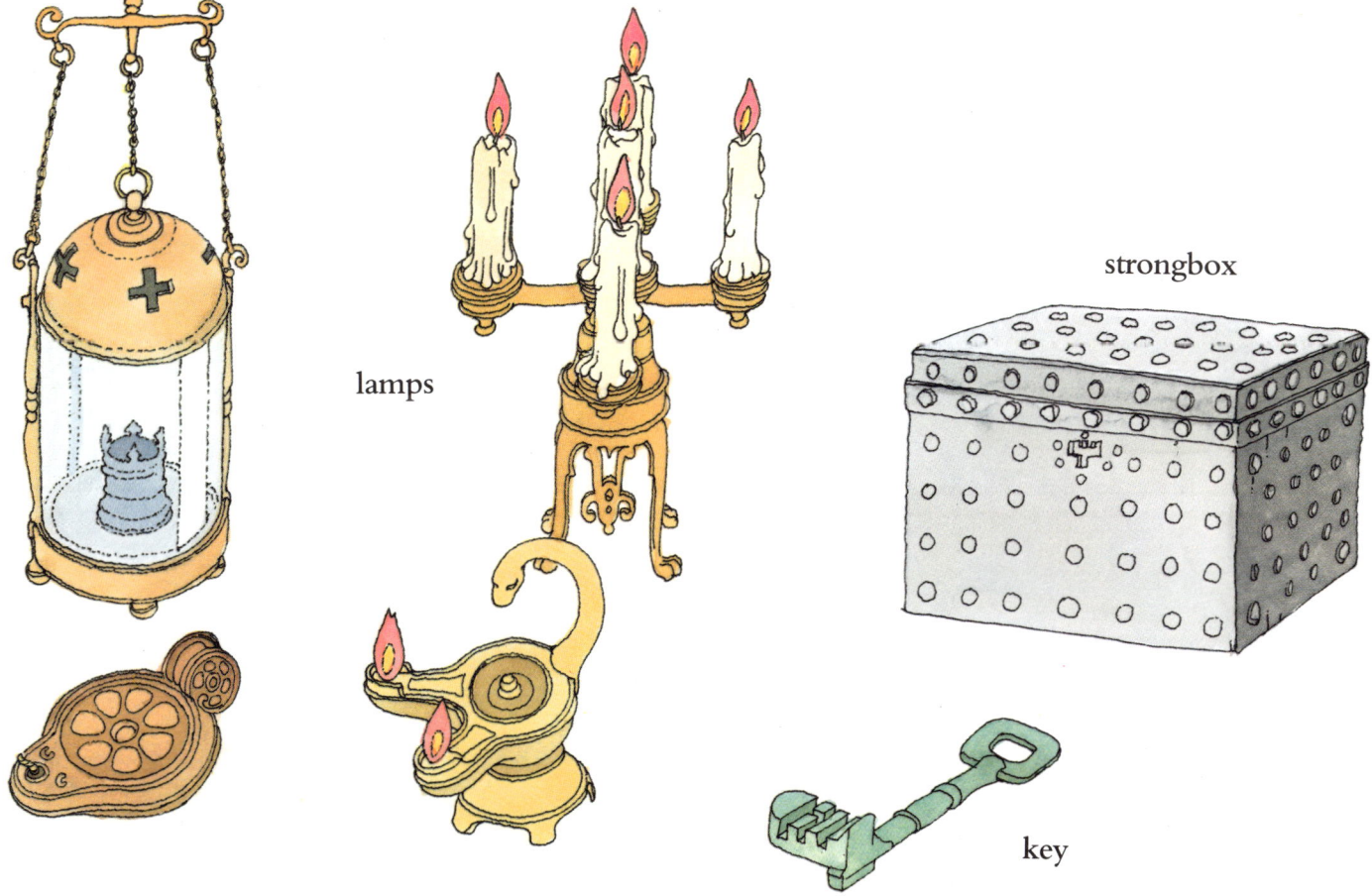

lamps

strongbox

key

potter's   butcher's   bar

Going shopping

The main street of Pompeii was known as the Street of Abundance. The Romans were famous for their road building, and this was a fine street, eight and a half metres wide. The pavements were broad and the road busy with carts and horses.

The street was always bustling, thronged with beggars and rich people, slaves running errands, musicians and jugglers, and men and women going shopping. There were all kinds of shops.

The owner was normally a freedman, that is a slave who had been given his freedom. He often lived with his family over the shop. The shop assistants were often slaves and young children.

Food to be sold was on display outside the shop, or stored inside in baskets or cool earthenware jars. It was difficult to keep things fresh without refrigeration. As people crowded into the shops there would be thieving and haggling and arguments. Cloth would be measured out with a ruler; vegetables would be weighed on the scales.

After a day's hard bargaining, merchants and traders from other towns might call by at a tavern or a bar for a drink. They would be offered the best wine of the region, or a bite to eat. In the taverns you could eat a proper meal, either lying on couches or sitting up on benches. At the entrance to the bar the customer would find a large counter made of coloured marble. Sunk into the marble were big earthenware pots containing the food and wine. If you drank too much you could always stay the night. Above the taverns there would be rooms for rent.

Barbers, butchers, bakers, pottery and hardware stores, wine merchants, carpenters and greengrocers... there was something for everyone on the Street of Abundance.

greengrocer's   barber's   wine merchant's

carpenter's

Pompeii at work

The archaeologist is not just a treasure hunter. One of the most incredible finds at Pompeii was not of gold or silver. It wasn't a priceless wall painting or statue. It was a bakery, and it was discovered by Giuseppe Fiorelli.

He opened up the room and dug with his bare hands until he found the oven. It had been so well sealed that no ash had got into it at all. Inside the oven he found 81 loaves. They were as hard as stone of course, but then they were 1,800 years old!

The loaves were round, with eight notches in the crust. Exactly the same kind of loaf was still being baked in Naples in Fiorelli's day! As excavations continued, more bakeries were found. There were more than 40 of them in

Pompeii, which suggests to us that people did not bake their own bread at home.

If bread was mass produced, how did bakers manage without steam or electric power? In the centre of the bakery was a large millstone which was dragged round and round by a pony or a donkey. Here the wheat was ground into flour.

The dough would be mixed and kneaded in a back room. It would then be left to stand for a few hours in a cool place. It was then taken to the ovens. These were wood-fired, with a pipe to carry away the smoke rather than a proper flue. When the tiles were white hot, the baker would push the embers to one side, and put in the loaves. He used a wooden shovel with a long handle.

Another important industry which required a lot of work was the manufacture of cloth. The Pompeians spun their yarn on spindles and wove their cloth on hand looms. After this the cloth would have to be 'finished' to make it smooth and even. Today this process is carried out by machines.

In Pompeii, as in 19th century Britain, the first stage of the 'finishing' of cloth was to soak it in urine. It was a practical system – and very cheap! Indeed, there were special urinals in the street, and passers-by were invited to contribute! After this the cloth would be treated with fuller's earth (a sort of clay) to get the grease out of it. It was then beaten, washed and napped.

It is hardly surprising that textiles were very expensive in Pompeii. A garment had to last for years and years. If you wanted a change of colour, however, you could always have it dyed! There were many dyers in Pompeii. The dyes were mixed up from vegetable and animal products, and placed in big vats. Here the textiles would be trampled underfoot, before being rinsed and hung out to dry.

People of Pompeii

Pompeii was part of the most powerful empire the world had ever seen. It traded over a very wide area. Its roads crossed the known world. Rome, the capital city, probably had a population of two million. In many ways the Roman world was like that of modern Europe. The more we see of life in Pompeii, the more familiar it seems to us.

Roman society was complicated and highly organized. Workers in different jobs were members of special guilds: dyers, bakers, goldsmiths, confectioners, barbers, shoemakers, perfumers and so on. Come election time the different guilds would support different candidates.

Slogans would be scrawled up on the walls of buildings, as today: 'Vote for Gaius Rufus, A Really Honest Man!', or 'Gaius Secundus Makes Good Bread – He'll Make a Good Administrator Too!'.

Some people made their living from writing slogans. At night they would sneak along the streets, carrying a ladder and a lantern. One would nip up the ladder to paint the slogan, while the other one held up a lantern so that they could see. The most famous of these publicists was called *Emilius Celer* – or 'Speedy Emilius'! One might almost say that he started the world's first advertising agency.

The streets of Pompeii would have been filled with people from all levels of society and all parts of the empire. As today, you would have been able to recognise most people by the way they looked. There would be centurions in scarlet cloaks, a senator in his official toga (gown), a drunken sailor, a pale noblewoman covered in jewellery, a tanned country woman selling eggs.

When we look at the ruins of Pompeii today we can see that modern Europe has its beginnings in ancient Rome. Roman civilisation spread over most of Europe. When the empire finally collapsed there were centuries of chaos and fighting. The towns the Romans built fell into ruin and disappeared. However the people of Europe never quite forgot the laws and customs of ancient Rome.

senator   magistrate   nobleman   noblewoman   young man

centurion   soldier   soldier   workman   shepherd

actor   merchant   dancer   country woman   peasant

gladiator   gladiator   gladiator   nurse and baby   smith

The rumbling mountain

The summer of AD 79 was normal enough in the town of Pompeii. There were the usual dinner parties, and fights in the amphitheatre. Visitors arrived from Rome and admired the peaceful countryside. The townspeople took Vesuvius for granted. They had never even chosen it as a subject for a wall painting.

Many people remembered the earthquake of AD 62, which had destroyed the town. However they did not connect it with Vesuvius. Today we know that the earthquake had in fact been caused by the mountain. Underground gases building up inside Vesuvius had failed to blow the top off the mountain. Instead they had spread underground, causing violent earth tremors.

People knew nothing about the science which today we call 'seismology' – the study of earthquakes. They thought that the gods must have been angry with them for some reason. However in August AD 79 people began to wonder again. There were slight earth tremors, and strange rumbling noises came from Vesuvius. Despite the fine weather, the sea was often rough.

On the morning of 24 August the animals in the farms around the city began to act strangely. Dogs howled and horses became restless. Suddenly there was a violent earth tremor. As people picked themselves up they stared towards Vesuvius in horror.

The peak of the mountain was splitting apart! To the sound of rumbles and crashes, a gigantic tongue of flame appeared. To the people of Pompeii it seemed as if they were standing at the gates of hell.

This time the underground gases had blown the top off the mountain. A thick hail of stones and cinders began to rain down, blotting out the sun. It was as if darkest night had fallen. Flashes of light showed people running for shelter or trying to escape. It was hopeless. For miles around the air was choking and the land was being swallowed up by ash. The eruption had begun.

The eruption

A torrent of boiling mud began to flow from Vesuvius. The villas on its slopes were engulfed as the mud rolled on towards the coast – to the small town of Herculaneum. The people who lived there fled in terror, leaving everything behind. Most of them managed to get away.

Lying off Misenum, 25 kilometres to the northwest, was the Roman fleet. The ships were under the command of a famous Roman called Gaius Plinius Secundus. We know him as Pliny the Elder, a famous soldier, writer and naturalist.

Seeing the eruption of Vesuvius, Pliny had the fleet weigh anchor and sail towards the disaster area. As a scientist, Pliny was fascinated by the eruption. As an important official, he had to try to help those who were in trouble.

Soon the ships were in serious difficulties themselves. Pumice rained down from the sky, and the sea was seething. Pliny turned towards Stabiae.

Here too the scene was terrible. The beach was littered with dead animals and fishes. People ran to and fro with burning torches. Huge breakers battered the beach, and the earth shook repeatedly. All day long the ashes poured down. Pliny went in search of a friend who lived in Stabiae. That night, after a particularly violent earth tremor, Pliny and his friend fled to the beach. The fleet had vanished. The waves were the size of houses, and the air was unbreathable. The great man started choking and coughing, and finally collapsed, dead.

Meanwhile in Pompeii people had barricaded themselves in their houses, hoping that the storm of ashes would soon be over. They hid in cellars and underground passages, but the fine ash filtered in everywhere. Poisonous fumes made them choke and gasp for air.

They realised too late that they were trapped. Grabbing their valuables, they made a dash for the streets. It was hopeless. They stumbled and fell against each other. Soon the road was blocked with fallen bodies and overturned carts.

The last hours

Pompeii was going through its death throes. The dust and stones formed huge drifts, up to eight metres high in places. The streets stank of sulphur from the volcano. One by one the lanterns of those trying to flee went out. Soon the only light was from flashes of lightning, and from the huge tongues of flame which still leapt from the crater of Vesuvius.

The lucky ones did manage to escape. The ones who did not lay buried in the ash, suffocated by fumes. The last hours of the town remain, recorded in the tuff for all time.

The archaeologists found saucepans on stoves, meat roasting in a bronze pan. A mother was covering her little girl with a shawl, vainly trying to save her life. Here were two girls who wasted time collecting up their jewellery, poisoned by the gas. Here were four women barricaded in their room.

Dozens of gladiators died because they were locked in their barracks. The guard must have fled with the keys, saving his own skin. In one house a funeral banquet was being held, to honour a dead friend. The guests themselves were soon to die as well.

In a temple, priests were making a sacrifice to the gods. They believed that the gods must be angry with them. Perhaps they could stop the disaster even now. Their prayers went unanswered, and they too choked to death. Vesuvius could not be placated.

The buried city

The eruption continued all the next day. For miles around not a living soul was to be found. At dawn on the third day, the wind began to break up the great black cloud covering the area. A pale sun rose to reveal a chilling scene.

To the south of Vesuvius the countryside was covered with a light grey ash. The force of the eruption may be indicated by the fact that ash from Vesuvius was carried southwards to the coast of north Africa and eastwards as far as Egypt and Syria. There was not a house left standing, not a tree or a blade of grass.

Some who had escaped returned to the area. They clawed at the ashes, but there was no point. When they looked up at the mountain which had revealed its terrible secret, they were stunned. Vesuvius was unrecognisable. Its green peak had been completely blasted away. Its slopes were now thick with grey lava. The mountainside had collapsed inwards, forming a crater some 11 kilometres across.

We shall never know just how many people died in the eruption. There must have been at least 2,000 in Pompeii alone. The story of the disaster spread to Rome and the furthest corners of the empire. Everybody was stunned.

Pompeii was never rebuilt. Over the centuries grass and bushes grew back over the wasteland. Vesuvius continued to rumble and roar from time to time, changing its shape yet again.

Marble and bricks lying above the soil were broken off and used in farm buildings. Only a slight oval-shaped hollow marked the former site of the amphitheatre, where once the crowds had cheered on the gladiators. No other trace remained. For 17 centuries Pompeii lay buried and forgotten.